AF351385

To the warmth
of the heart

João Quintino Silva

To the warmth of the heart

Period: 2000 - 2009
1st. Edition

Belo Horizonte – Minas Gerais
2022

To the warmth
of the heart

2022 © JOÃO QUINTINO SILVA

Editor
João Quintino Silva

Artwork and drawings
Aderivaldo Santos

Cataloging Form

Silva, John Quintin, 1934–

S586   To the warmth of the heart: period: 2000 – 2009 / João Quintino Silva. – 1. ed.– Belo Horizonte: Author's Ed, 2022.
126 p.

1.Brazilian Poetry I.Title.

CDD: B869.15

Responsible librarian:
Cleide A. Fernandes CRB6 / 2334

This book is for sale on the website:
www.amazon.com – www.amazon.com.br
https://clubedeautores.com.br

Contacts with the author:
jqs.poeta@gmail.com

2022
All rights reserved

"That's why who loves, who feels in the chest
Sing him the lyre the best,
The carmes hear them, that the bards only sing
Miss you, perfumes, raptures and love! "

Antonio Gonçalves Dias

(Last Corners — The Golden Cloud, p. 183)

SUMMARY

Author's Works

- Basket of Rhymes – Sonnets

- Verses of My Affection

- Musal

- To the Warmth of the Heart

- My Soul Sings

- Love Poems and Other Motives

- One Verse, Another Verse...

- Childhood Smell – Reminiscence

- Earth-Earth

- Genetliac Poems – Happy Birthday

- Wedding, Many Weddings

- Poems and Texts from the Greater Time

- Sevensyllabic rounds

- Of Friendship (Text in Prose and Verse)

- On the Art of Writing – Observations

- Tracks of My Fist

João Quintino and Irvalda

Biographical Overview

JOÃO QUINTINO SILVA, son of UBERABA-MG, with birthday on October 31, has, by parents, JOÃO ANTÔNIO SILVA and BENEDICTA COSTA E SILVA.

Married to IRVALDA ALVES REZENDE.

Children: MARCOS RICARDO RESENDE SILVA, Lawyer, married to REGINA VELOSO HORTA, Economiária;

MARINEZ REZENDE OLIVEIRA, married to DIMAS DE LIGÓRIO OLIVEIRA, INSS Auditor;

MARCELO REZENDE SILVA, Master of Taekwondo, Businessman, married to Dentist DERLAINE LOPES.

Grandchildren:

JOÃO PEDRO,

OTÁVIO REZENDE,

JOÃO GABRIEL,

MARIA EDUARDA,

ANA VITÓRIA,

DANIEL LOPES.

He worked in the Magisterium in the Cities of Uberaba, Uberlândia, Nova Ponte, Monte Alegre, Belo Vale, Monte Carmelo, in the latter exercising the position of Director of the Juscelino Kubitschek College. He experienced Higher Magisterium at Sete Lagoas Law School, eventually, and in preparatory courses.

He worked as a Career Magistrate in the Minas Gerais district of Belo Vale, Campina Verde, Iturama, Oliveira, Belo Horizonte. He was a member of the Court of Appeals and the Judge of the Court of Justice of the State of Minas Gerais. In all counties, he served as Electoral Judge cumulatively.

Effective Member and Former President of ARCÁDIA DE MINAS GERAIS, Effective Member of the MUNICIPALIST ACADEMY OF LETTERS OF MINAS GERAIS. He had a visit to the BRAZILIAN UNION TROVERS, section of Minas Gerais.

He occupied literary space in the journal GAZETA de Minas Gerais, by Oliveira, and in Jornal de Casa, by BH; Jornal Decision columnist, editor-in-chief and participant of Magiscultura Magazine, both of the Minas Gerais Magistrates Association.

Some lifetime awards and honors.

PREFACE

When the muses choose their elect, they place little stars on their foreheads in their wombs. These privileged grow up with a different look at the world, glimpse beyond what most mortals perceive. With the sensibility of their skin, they transcend the real and connect with the sacred, in a symbiosis that drives them to share a trapped treasure eager to explode.

Not only the written words of poets portray the beauty of feelings. Anyone who reads or listens to them understands that beyond the formal meaning, some halo illuminates the simple set of letters.

And the poetry comes out of a cauldron, stewed in cooking for life. In the youth, next to the clear water harvested in a nearby source, it adds love, dream, hope, chimeras....

Time passing, the muses, with their demanding taste, threaten to throw the stew into the fire. The poet-cook has two alternatives: making new broth, fetching water from a more reliable source, measuring in the balance needs the same ingredients, add new, or otherwise economical, fix the almost done delicacy. Way and choice of each. Maybe wine to color, starch to bend, exotic herbs guaranteeing a bright aroma? So learn the secrets of good taste, the right measure, the point of salt.

And becomes a master!

No longer need to measure, experienced hands hit a simple touch or look.

I don't know what steps the author of this book went through, but at one point there is no discussion: when he was born, parents may not have seen it, but there was a little star on his forehead. It was bestowed by the muses.

Today is a master!

When our dear confrere of Arcadia of Minas Gerais, **Judge João Quintino Silva**, proposed to me to write this preface, I felt honored and accepted the task with joy. He already knew his lines, spacially. And admired them. Gathered in this book, I read them in one breath, couldn't stop. My admiration increased.

Several thoughts occurred to me while reading:

He describes himself as a poor boy born in the interior of Minas Gerais. The first contact with poetry, I imagine, was attention to the singing of birds, the hue of flowers, the running of ants, tree branches dancing in the wind. He must have observed the clouds in their shifting evolution over the blue sky. It certainly created stories. The first verses, if not passed to paper, were the root of the beauties that the brain built and graced the boy's enchantment in the face of life's discoveries.

Teen, of course, found himself a poet. Stanzas sprang

up on themes like the first love and dreams to come true. Or the first disappointment... who doesn't have them?

Did you suffer?

It has been said that the poet is only great if he suffers ...

Hey balls! So verses only make sense when they rhyme love and pain? With regrets, unpleasantness, unhappiness?

Our poet, **Dr. João Quintino Silva,** presents us in this book with poetry full of optimism, mature, from someone who has already overcome uncertainties. Sell wisdom. Not once does the whining, on the contrary, sings the beauty of life, love, friendship: MY KINGDOM FOR A MINI VERSE

Why not

A minhon verse

Little one,

Squeezed in a drop of inspiration?

Such a verse of tenderness,

Of good will;

That little that says it all,

Synthesis of magic,

Lint of any atom;

That little thing,

Concentrated,

Microscopic

Able, however,

To explode in cascades of love

In the flow of deep thought metrics and rhymes: "THE WORD"

"A handful of letters – the word

But the word dissorse in verse

Flee from the ephemeral of the slave mind

And it reaches the fullness of the universe. "

to the simplicity of everyday life: CHEESE BREAD

I felt the still life

Tasting this delicacy

That with earthenware tea,

It was the charm of my day.

The optimism present in each stanza shows that our poet lives the fullness of life, reaps the fruits of the fruitful journey, of professional fulfillment, on the pillar of duty accomplished. Someone's verses of good with the world.

Pains of love? Nothing! Found in the gentle Irvalda the perfect companion, present, loving, inspiring muse, foundation: I AND HER

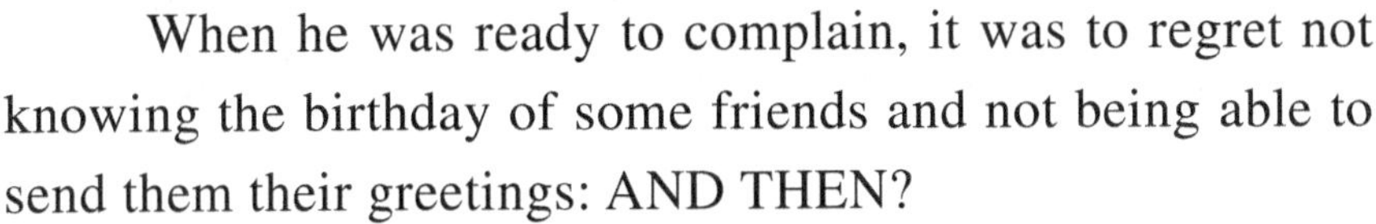

João and Irvalda,
Both of us,
Holding hands,
Naughty looks,
Smiles – Ripe Fruits
Coming out of the mouth ...
– Promises of unforgettable night.

When he was ready to complain, it was to regret not knowing the birthday of some friends and not being able to send them their greetings: AND THEN?

Ungrateful life I'm leading,
Between doubts and mistakes,
Because I never knew when
My friends are years old.

If you talk about death, treat it lightly, don't play poor. On the contrary, it gives the subject a Gaiata connotation, as in: "MY TIME TO DIE"

"They will say of me,
Seeing my inert body
On a cold platform,
Ornate Flower and Candlelight:
– "Poor guy: it was so good!..."

Thus, in verses impregnated with lyricism, sensitivity and lucidity, our Judge-Poet fulfills the vocation:

"GRANDMA old lady"
"The third is worn out
From running around so much"

The serenity that Dr. Quintino distributes is the result of his professional career because he knew how to combine the aridity of codes with the absolute poetics of law. In the seriousness of courts, a judge fulfilling the law with the tenderness of the poet, practicing justice as the sublime ideal.

Marilene Guzella Martins Lemos
Pedagogue - Storyteller - Chronicler - Essayist -
Writer - President of the Arcadia of Minas Gerais -
President of the Friends of Culture Academy -
Member of the Municipalist Academy of Letters of Minas Gerais -
Member of the Historical and Geographic Institute of Minas
Gerais - Member of the Minas Gerais Women's Academy of Letters
- Member of the Minas Gerais Lionism Academy.

THE MIME
THAT GIVE YOU

Today I do not bring you flowers.
I bring you the virgin palm
Of the glory that is mine and yours.
I bring you in flower your own soul,
Garden where flowers and estua
The expression of my loves.

———————

MORNING-NIGHT CHUVARENTA

Washed from heavy rain,
That still falls – smooth, now –
The houses boasts
A bizarre look of cleanliness.

Behind the multicolored skyscrapers
And of various architecture,
Point – taller –
The ridges of Serra do Curral,
In an all-green sovereign spreads,
Uniting heaven and earth,
As a symbol of hope.

February – 2000

TWO INFINITE
(Jacaraípe Beach)

Green waters, blue sky:

Two infinites!

Between them,

Wind in plated,

Light dress

– Living portion

Of the holy creation

I dream the imponderable

And immerse yourself in the beauty of everything,

In the solemn beauty of everything!

————————

February 21 – 2000

João Quintino Silva

BEACH IS BEACH

Beach is beach!
Sea is sea!
The delight of a sand,
Seeing the sun that faints beyond,
It gives pleasure and makes you dream.

———————

February – 2001

LOVE NOMADE

From the bottom of the mysteries,
Under orchestral seresta d'aves,
I landed in the colorful dawn
From the corners of UBERABA,
On OCTOBER 31
From a cosmically happy year.

Son of the Wind,
Rainbow dress
And with whispers of water,
Riding the hope,
I came across the world,
Restless, nomad,
Sure to find you,
O my life!
To together make up the world of happiness
That will be just the two of us!

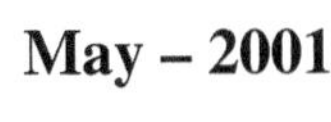

May – 2001

MY TIME TO DIE

My time to die will be all mine.
No one will want to take it.
It would have been a life of struggle,
Instantly,
For the conquest of paradise,
– The other life,
Eternal and ethereal,
No comedy and no confiscations,
No paid work,
Without uncertainty policy,
No risks of family stability.

They will say of me,
Seeing my inert body
On a cold platform,
Ornate Flower and Candlelight:
– "Poor guy! it was so good!..."

But you will never know that the good thing,
The good total, the good juicy and tasty
It was ideal,
In desire they will of the earth,
Because perfection in love
It is the endless and the beginningless,
The pure abstract
that doesn't fit in the concave space
From a simple heart.

November 2001

MARIA – MARIA

There are so many Marys,
In the popular malice ...
Maria-mole,
Smoke mary,
Wafer Mary,
Maria-mijona,
Maria-stirs-angu,
Maria-go-with-the-others ...

But,
A Mary exists,
Every one infests such debauchery:
– The Mary of my heart!

October – 2002

MINERAL AGGREGATE

Body,
Mineral Aggregate
Which returns to dust.

First,
The capricious nature makes us.
Give us a taste of the world
And in the end,
At the same dust,
To the dust we were before
Will make us return.

October – 2002

BRIEF LIFE –
TEMPUS FUGIT

Whole life,
The great life
It's like the half hour of the clock:
Pass soon.

It is the disconsolation of lost time,
The bitterness of misunderstood luck,
The ideal that found no realization.

Life is like an iron train,

That for a moment in the weather station

And that disappears,

Five minutes later,

Behind the first corner,

Just leaving, for remembrance,

The whistle noise,

The bumps of history,

The snort of the iron heart.

Life has

The duration of a breath,

The brevity of a wink,

The volatile consistency of a soap bubble,

The almost nothing of a closed circle.

The Train of Life

Pass soon.

October – 2002

EVA DAUGHTER

Woman...
Vector body,
Lines as
The divine imagination!
Rising lines,
Down lines,
Misaligned lines,
Curves, Semicurves,
Short, long,
Bottles,
In admirable combination!

There! patterned curves,
Continuous,
Discontinuous
That in a do-it-yourself
But-don't-follow,
They point to infinity,
Hit wide eyes
And they pin the concupiscent heart!

Woman!
It's sweet to fall
In its colossal abysses
And in sins
Of your curvilinear mysteries!

November – 2002

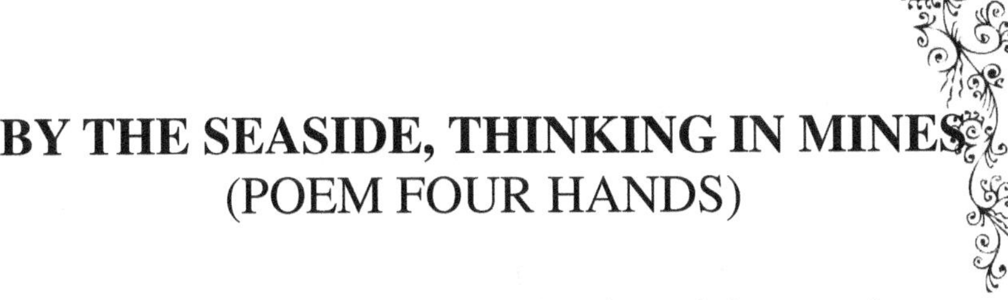

BY THE SEASIDE, THINKING IN MINES
(POEM FOUR HANDS)

Dr. Moacir Rodrigues and
João Quintino Silva

This sea, green and deep,

That overflows in half world,

Trapped by colossal chasms,

Cry sometimes (tells the story),

For never having the glory

To bathe MINAS GERAIS!

We have no sea in Minas

For the girls' gaudy

It is not harmful to us,

Because we have - refreshment -

All the iron in the hemisphere,

Rich and coveted soil.

Our blondes and brunettes
They provide beautiful scenes
In the eyes of everyone.
They are more beautiful than beauty
That offers nature
From this deep green sea.

To say without exaggeration:
In the miner's pipe
There's a throbbing mass
Fruitful in science and art,
– which is a model everywhere,
– That the whole of Brazil imitates.

December 17 - 2,002
(Vila Velha)

THE GOOD VERSE

The good verse
There has to be music in between,
Softness of dry leaf in the wind,
Rhythm Overture
That takes the body rock
And the fascination of the soul.

You have to remember "longing",
Beautiful woman smile
Loose in the pleasure of living,
This kind of human that looks the most
The subtle painting of a Rembrandt,
Who ran away from the screen
To come wrap in our gaze.

The good verse
It has to have mystery,
Evocation.

Have to suggest
Beyond Concrete Language
And from rational graphics,
In a symbolism
That only the heart (not the mind)
Will be able to understand.

You have to sing life,
The dream,
Love,
The fraternity,
- God, in the center of everything,
And the man at his feet,
In worship
And ecstasy.

———————

March - 2003

GESTUARIA

Gestures ...

We all have gestures.
If it's love,
They will be worth it,
Because love consecrates,
Love unites,
Love redeems,
Love coexists and shares,
Love balances the universe.

In the symbiosis of love, two grow:
To be lover
And being loved,
And wins the world
A harmony, which does not perish,
Never.

———————

March - 2003

João Quintino Silva

POETRY IS SO

Going down
From a romantic crackle
From my parents.

Parade for life
In a fight
Where the weapon is the acute spirit
What, fencing
Penetrates deep into the sensitivity
And catch
Loving Smiles
And incentives of devotion.

I'm happy in this fight
Where the heart is called inspiration
And victory consists in generous applause
And constructive
Of human friendship.

POETRY is like this.
Another thing to be should not:
– A whole audience that reads...
– A poet who writes to you.

———————

April - 2003

MATURITY

I live in health and hope,
Malgrade
Good account of the years.

I bent the mountain,
Which is broad-topped to me,
Grass green,
Golden sun,
Cheerful of birds,
Refreshing clear water.

I'm happy
In contemplating the other side,
Whose descent, I hope,
Be gentle to me
Like the smile of the newborn
And the cicle of the evening breeze.

———————

September – 2003

BOTH OF US
(Together for ever in love)

We are very happy
In this life of love,
No hurts, no slips ...
Strong – even in pain.

We have this address:
I live in it; she – in me ...
Together – from the beginning,
Together until the end.

October – 2003

POEM OF CREATION

The night was so black,
So dense
That weighed on the skin,
It hurt the eyes,
– Mass compact of piche!

The night sky ...
No star,
No moonlight,
No light

I, plunged into fog,
Faced with an unfinished universe,
I went back to the creation of the world.

It was when GOD appeared,
Whose powerful voice called out:
– "FIAT LUX!"
And the earth was flooded
Of delicious clarity,
Of joy and celebration,
Warming my heart!

———

February - 2004

BEING NOCTURNAL

I like to see nature sleeping,
The night itself,
The time,
In this hour of silence and fear,
– Fear of darkness and loneliness.

I stay
(Only guardian of life)
The schism,
By measuring the firmament with the eyes,
Counting the stars trembling and small
And the footsteps of the moon
On your sidereal ride.

Eu olho para o perfil cinza das montanhas
Num círculo
Trapaça Verde Vegetal,
Limitando meu mundo ...

Eu divido a massa multigeométrica das casas
Insinuando o abrigo de quem dorme ...

Eu ouço uma voz perdida,
Mais sussurros do vento
Nas galerias da rua ...

À noite, vestido de sombra,
Eu vibro profundamente,
Eu escuto a inspiração transgressora
E eu deixei meus versos vazarem
Nas páginas gentis dessa música!

———————

Fevereiro - 2004

TO THE CABLE
NELCI MARTINS SOARES

Congratulations, CABLE NELCI,

From the notes I read today

In our last newspaper,

Where the Egregious Court,

Without doing any favors,

Recognize its value

Guardian of our peace,

The impeccable cop

Which, estimated on the spot,

Does so well all you do.

———————

May 18 - 2004

45

João Quintino Silva

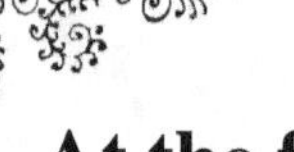

At the foot of SERRA DO CURRAL

The deep blue

It's a screen exposed in the sky,

Flaunt white brush strokes

Here and there...

It's a dome

Supported by the green curves of SERRA DO CURRAL

Which comprises below

The portentous house,

The tall buildings,

The white-walled houses,

We rushed from the streets,

The queued cars,

The careless children,

Myself - and everything

Which makes up a shaking metropolis,

Including faith,

The dream,

Love!

————————

16 - 06 - 2004

ME AND HER

João and Irvalda,
Both of us.
Holding hands,
Naughty looks,
Smiles – Ripe Fruits
Falling from the mouth...
– Promises of unforgettable night.

The earth is the catwalk
In which we parade,
In the eyes of all,
Our way of being happy.

———

18 - 06 - 2004

JOÃO QUINTINO SILVA

SMALL WORD

One small word,
Monosyllabic,
Without phonetic weight,
But that sustains
All the dream in the world:
– PEACE!

––––––––––

20 – 06 – 2004

BE MUTANT
**To the most distinguished
Mrs. ACÁCIA BARRETO DA MOTTA MESSANI
(in memoriam)**

Earth people,
I did not die!
I became homesick!
Now,
I'm an ethereal angel
Wrapped in infinity.
I am more alive than ever.
The contradictions of the world cut my being,
They freed my essence.

To be is to be
Never goes extinct,
Death is simply a change of appearance.
Lavoisier was right:
"In nature,
Nothing is created,
Nothing is lost;
Everything changes".

Now, free from the human carcass,
Light,
Volatile,
Transparent,
I am an enlightened being
In the heavens of eternity.

———

30 – 09 – 2004

49

JOÃO QUINTINO SILVA

WHERE IS MINAS?

Where is MINAS?
When far away, in remembrance.
Anywhere
In the heart.

I do not change Minas Gerais
In another corner.
Here I was born.
Here I will be reborn.
My cradle of gold and diamond.

My MINAS GERAIS!
The Mines of all good!
The Mines that adorn the "World Map"!
Mines that give higher content
To the history of Brazil!

Love territory,
Fatherland of Freedom,
MINAS is here,
– In our hearts!

25 – 10 – 2004

FULL MOON

Full moon,

Night sky,

– The soul overflowing with light...

What a happy omen

Made me contemplative like that?!

I had wished, hands raising, O moon!

Caress you to the Argentine

And paint, with your light,

The dark bowels of my heart!

---

28 – 04 – 2005

João Quintino Silva

TO CAPTAIN
JOSÉ CARLOS BORGES

Congratulations, CAPTAIN BORGES,
By the highest rank
That enriches your saddlebag
And flatter your people!

Congratulations to RITA – the shrewd,
From whom has come, throughout history,
The incentive to fight
That gave you this victory.

Be happy in the high rank,
Earning a thousand
In the mission of great pleasure
That the gallon gave you.

Be happy in your future,
Votes are from IRVALDA AND JOÃO,
Very honored to own
A nephew CAPTAIN!

October 17 - 2005

MY EYES WALKED IN
INFINITE BLUE FAR

I liked the evolution of New Moon,

In the old night of my dream.

It was like a chalk,

By outer magic,

were filling her curve and shine

Until there is no space left without light.

– It's the kingdom of the full moon,

Charming lady of the night,

Delicate pin from my eyes,

Intoxicating plenum!

———

12 - 11 - 2005

COSMIC JEALOUSY

I don't want astronauts in space
In moon script.

I don't want telescopes
Lifting the inquiring lens and steel halo
Against plenilunios and solstices.

I don't want lunar rockets,
Wandering Astrophysicists
In light-year calculations.

I do not want.
– The moon is a privilege of the poet.

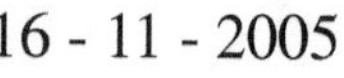

16 - 11 - 2005

TO PAINTERS OF INTEGRAMAGIS

TO PAINT! Sun that enchants the views!
Virtue God offers
To open-minded people
How are our artists.

I see in all such inclinations,
Light hands so calibrated
That from your brush strokes,
Forms arise, flowers are born.

Deserve our praises
For the charm of these screens
Which demonstrate, flowing from them,
Real talent for colors!

———

27 - 11 - 2,005

JOÃO QUINTINO SILVA

VARIATIONS ABOUT KISS

To my taste,
The kiss is sweet
As if it were
Honeycomb.

Yeah, please,
When well given,
The sacred link
Of the union of love.

Stolen kiss,
Middle awkward
And per defect
Very rushed.

Own to the vampire
– Bandit act –
Bitten kiss
Cuts sigh.

Two much in order,
Kiss in the dark
It's safe act:
Never ends.

———————

2 - 01 - 2006

READING MERCES MARIA MOREIRA

I smell roses in my way

And the great grace to see you

Dancing in the mild wind,

Suspended in the air,

Trapped only by light wires

From the sun that lights up my tropical dawn.

Good to see you,

Heaven's Aspiration,

The master talent of the earth,

The hand that weaves wonders,

The fist embroidering the dream in rhymes,

The heart that transforms the word

In verse - jewel of rare splendor.

—————

January 9 - 2006

READING "THE FLOWERS OF WORLD FOR YOU " FROM MERCES MARIA MOREIRA LOPES

MERCÊS – Goddess of Rhymes
(Fact without any secret),
Makes pain masterpieces,
Make the verses a toy.

Has repeated reading
Every book she made.
Dawn sun for life,
– It's nice to read MERCES.

Grateful for the courtesy
Shipping this time.
A charm of poetry
"THE FLOWERS .... FOR YOU".

January 12 - 2006

What about
GERALDO FERREIRA LIMA?

How good is GERALDO LIMA
And Mrs. LUCIA – Lady one hundred percent –
For which I cherish a deep esteem,
Whom for more news am I watching ?!

———

25 - 3 - 2006

A VOTES
HAPPY EASTER

Gratitude for the letter
Whose content tells us
Intentions of living grace
For a HAPPY EASTER.

I want them EASTER, too,
Just marked tenderness,
Filled with the light that suits
To a blessed FAMILY.

---

19 - 04 - 2006

JULY HOROSCOPE

TOURINA is very smart;
But rude in its mysteries.
LEONINA is more open,
The most docile of women.

LEONINA has malice,
Much more than another woman.
With a knack and skill,
Sling everything you want.

Although the meek eyes,
In a calm that suits,
She's mad at other hauls
Like when someone offends you.

With the look like a brazier,
Without disguise of intention,
Taking a very good leap,
She chokes the intruder.

———

20 - 04 - 2006

JOÃO QUINTINO SILVA

OLD GRANDMA

Her third is worn out
From running the accounts so much.

Praying
Ask for me,
For us,
For the peace of the world.

It's sweet to look at her
On your grandmother's throne,
Commander of four generations.
Little people,
The withered body,
Squeezed,
Condensed by the force of years,

Sin Free
And ambitions,
Full of peace and devotion;
Light as feather,
More in heaven than on earth,
– That is the best abode of holy souls there...

In the small hands,
The fingers almost fleshless,
Dresses like gloves rather than fur,
They are thrashing the godly accounts
While your withered lips
Whisper
Your prayers of fervor,
Short and in a hurry
As one who is afraid
Of the sudden interruption of death!

28 - 4 - 2006

JOÃO QUINTINO SILVA

WINTER IN YOUR ARMS

Bent to tiredness,
In the cold winter,
My stray body
Nestle in your arms.

Not being like this,
Your divine lap
Warms up the boy
That lives in my chest.

Happy – no fear –
I sleep, smiling,
Dreaming the most beautiful
From the dreams of love.

———————

5 - 05 - 2006

POETESS
EURIDES LACERDA FLECHA
(Acrostic)

EURIDES, great person,
A lady of talent,
Rare voice that sounds to heaven,
Light Sister by one hundred percent,
I leave a verse at your command
And I keep wishing
His trova, which is so good!

———————

16 - 05 - 2006

THANK YOU
(To Poet Eurides Lacerda Arrow)

Thank you, Dona EURIDES,
Your ACROSTIC for me,
Result of golden lides
Which happily put me like that!

Cheers don't deserve it
This humble poet
Whose verse is only prayer
Freed from the restless soul.

Your rhymes of high appreciation,
Focusing on what I live,
They say more than I deserve.
– I'll keep it as an incentive.

———————

26 - 05 - 2006

AND THEN?

Ungrateful life I'm leading,
Between doubts and mistakes,
Because I never knew when
My friends are years old.

If friendship is priceless,
For the record in my binder,
Give me an address,
Day and month of birthday.

Aware, therefore, of the age event,
As a friend always attentive,
I will have my own verse and various
For the pleasure of a greeting.

———————

May 29 - 2006

João Quintino Silva

A MESSAGE

What a perfect disappearance,
Dear CURSED friend!
Snail is like this,
Inside the bark, isolated.

Certainly, health is good,
Without showing disturbance.
However, time flies
Without giving information.

It can be anytime,
In writing or out loud,
Without the slightest delay,
Send a "hi" ... a "hi" to us!

———

9 - 06 - 2006

GRATITUDE

(To the Zeni poets of Barros Lana and
Célia Maria Barbosa Rodrigues)

Thanks for the access
To this "TROVY WORKSHOP",
Edition that successfully
Fits us in new rules.

Broadening the narrow mind,
Your book cheers us up
Seeing in the elected thunder
One care the most rhyme.

———————

15 - 06 - 2006

JOÃO QUINTINO SILVA

MY POETIC GLOSS

> "Black nights ... Loneliness ...
> Too late for both of them!
> A yes overriding a no ..
> And a "" maybe ""... for later! "
> (Célia Maria Barbosa Rodrigues)

"BLACK NIGHTS... LONELINESS..."
Your absence mistreats me,
It makes my affliction grow,
It drives me crazy... it almost kills!

Spring never comes
"TOO LATE FOR US TWO."
Long night never changes
The flash of afterglow.

To the song swings,
I want to have you in my arms.
"A YES CANNOT A NO"
Open to kisses more spaces.

I offered you perfect love
In a meeting of both of us.
It was a bad answer
"MAYBE... FOR LATER!"

———————

June 18 - 2006

IN FRONT OF A CALENDAR

YEAR...
Kid time,
Pass soon!

Pure illusion of irreverent calendar ...
Bird flight, in a short path,
From here to there,
Within which every dream
Play the endless blue
Where it dives forever and ever.

Time!
In a body that dies,
A dream that is reborn
Transfigured and resplendent.

July 26 - 2006

TO THE LAWYER
DR. JOSÉ FRANCISCO
THEOTÔNIO MACHADO

Dear Master Doctor JOSÉ MACHADO,
We thank you for the kind offer.
From Your Rhyming Book- A Find
That makes life an open window.

Good reading, we did together,
IRRALDA and JOÃO, this beautiful morning,
Very excited about the thousand subjects,
– Work that the tender dream gives us.

How beautiful the life of DOCTOR MACHADO!
Man of faith, perfect citizen!
Who as he lives will have granged
An unconditional admiration.

If we confront by the tone of the glow
DR. MACHADO GOLD OF GERAIS,
We will all see, without falling off the track,
May our illustrious friend SHINE MORE.

———

July 30 - 2006

THE WORD

A handful of letters - the word.
But the word, spoken in verse,
Flee from the ephemeral of the slave mind
And it reaches the fullness of the universe.

In the Dictionary's statement,
The WORD is like brick
Housed in a construction site.
Mere body of letters.
It does not reflect beauty,
Don't get excited
It does not move in the contemplative mystery.

When, however, tied to other elements,
In combined forms,
In fantastic syntax,
Like the brick between mortars,
Steel and iron jambs
Then stresses the strength of literary architecture
That enchants the eyes
And it animates the heart.

The WORD is not worth.
Worth the prose speech,
If it comes from reason;
From the back,
It proceeds from the soul.

---

31 - 07 - 2006

JOÃO QUINTINO SILVA

SARAU IN FRIENDSHIP PALACE (THE AGUIAR AX CLAN)

In the wide corner of life,
I look at DOCTOR MACHADO
Whose virtue invites
To a blessed living.

"LIFE AND LAWYERS 'VERSES"
It's bedside book
Read with great pleasure
All the time, the whole life.

My dear DOCTOR MACHADO,
The friendship that holds us
It is cut diamond.
You don't buy, you don't sell.

Be grateful to them only
By the invitation we made
To attend your party,
A FEST OF THAT WAY!

It was me and my IRVALDA,

My treasure, my fairy,

My emerald jewel,

My sweet and eternal beloved.

Lots of life, lots of hug...

High feedback corners...

Fine people in every space

Leaving everything beautiful.

It's ours DAMA NAZINHA,

Dedicated in a lot of eagerness,

In the most impeccable line,

More than perfect hostess.

CONGRATULATIONS TO THE FAMILY

Which showed how to do it

A PARTY that shines

Good taste, love, peace.

August 23 - 2006

João Quintino Silva

IRVALDA AND I – WE BOTH

I, in love, I'm doing well.
A success as I wanted.
I finally found someone
That makes me very happy.

Through prime verses,
I'm glad to announce
That the minute we met
Made us eternal pair.

You don't live well alone,
No matter how squirming:
It's mistér woman, affection,
In the union that makes the force.

Both of us, so well married,
Under the blessings of the Lord,
Walkers, arm in arm,
For eternity of love.

Our life of kindness,
Having me in it what I need,
It's not a dream – it's reality
With flavor of paradise.

———————
14 - October - 2006

BY CHANCE OF RHYMES

Eis meu poem expired
Transformed not suco
Of unthinkable delicacy.

Semente miúda
Da broto, vira muda
Pra florir meu pomar.

Rola-rola uma ball
Na escola green area
Grow up to jump.

To a gostoso payment
A pessoa não pode
Attend sem dançar.

I will hold na vala
Entupindo a room
What a year to give.

Dies or poor operator
Sem or ouvido of um dobre
When or how to bury.

Sobe ao Céu or caught,
Last year, released,
– What or Céu é seu place.

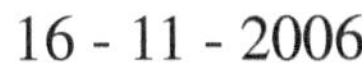

16 - 11 - 2006

JOÃO QUINTINO SILVA

DOUBT

I don't know what holds me the most,
If Curral da Serra
Where I put my bones, meat
And dreams,
Or if your heart
Where I planted my ideal of happiness
And where I see flourish
My own life.

———

20 - 11 - 2006

ZENI DE BARROS LANA
EDIT NEW BOOK

So good to read ZENI,
Like "GOD IN MY LIFE"!
All of her as I read
Pos my soul enraptured.

Focus the feeling well,
Express it with beauty
It is the task of a portent,
A primacy of royalty.

ZENI LANA – the portentosa –
Put in the writing, which is diverse,
A life in every prose,
One soul in each verse.

Light more light than a star,
Best carat gold,
Congratulations tell her
For the gifts that make her vate.

CONGRATULATIONS, dear ZENI,
For the gift you see there.
Intuition of how much I heard,
Everyone likes you.

2 - 12 - 2006

JOÃO QUINTINO SILVA

DECLINING ZENI
(Acrostic)

ZENI has a keen taste
In every verse that says.
Nothing escapes your care ...
Urges to listen to her and ask for bis.

———————

3 - 12 - 2006

READING ZENI LANA
"GOD IN MY LIFE", pags.129 / 130

Through the corners of life
Of ZENI only well spoken,
Cultured and applauded woman,
With heat in any room.

Talented our lady,
Whose I am in the verse brother,
Weaves poems that declaim
With the voice of the heart.

It's a woman with a lot of art,
Which one can see from your soiree.
It gets along everywhere.
Loves Beethoven, Strauss...

Having a softening laugh
(A mystery, like, any),
She is a most resembling being
Angel in the form of woman.

———————

7 - 12 - 2006

PREZADÍSSIMO
DOCTOR JOSÉ AMÂNIO

DESEMBARGADOR-POET,
Grateful to praise my cradle
Coa magic of an esthete
Who has a gift for singing and verse.

THE UBERABA BOY,
No wealth in your hand,
I wanted a good that is not over.
That is the formation of the school.

Faced hard setbacks
In this war to win,
Not often having
From a penny to eat.

It set off in the noisy world
Your fight never in vain,
So that the force of the straw
It guaranteed him this rise.

Ah! august and guapa victory,
That reached with fearlessness!
– Here is the honorable cloak
JUDGE-DESEMBARGADOR!

Not alone, because IRVALDA,
A splendid consort,
Who supports you, who supports you,
It made him see a clear NORTH.

———

09 - 12 - 2006

VIRTUAL WOMAN

Woman today, smart artist,
To your plural talent
Add another achievement:
– The one of VIRTUAL WOMAN.

On the Internet you surf,
The computer donzel
It is the beloved who gives himself
With love and all love.

She embraces that device
With such gallant care
Which remind me of sweet commitment
From the embrace of two lovers.

To the WA

The electronic device,
Which dominates verse and obverse,
Much more than a mirror,
Put the whole universe at its feet.

Diploma internet user,
Anything can this woman
That, in the faith with which you tame us,
Make us everything you want.

Never boredom or tiredness,
Which are always a horrible evil,
They shortened their spaces
To life towards the dream.

The INTERNET is a good thing
To the earthling on the trail.
– How we fly in it!...
– How good to rise to the stars!...

———

January 9 - 2007

85

JOÃO QUINTINO SILVA

TO THE POET COMPOSER
DESEMBARGADOR
JOSÉ AMÂNCIO DE SOUZA FILHO

Thank you the tribute
To my estrus – honorable gift –
And equally that message
All in verse, to the GOOD YEAR.

Gratitude is an exercise
Nice each time.
Not forget the benefit
That your song made me.

In this controversial world,
I'm happy with emotion
Seeing that in the verse theme
I now have a new brother.

What beauty impresses the rhyme
In the harmony of the song!
Full art that cheers me up
To the smiles of ovation.

I notice, therefore, that he is master in this
To take the rhyme
With strict commitment
To compose a masterpiece.

—————

January 11 - 2007

GENERATING POEM

Disguise the hurt
In one verse,
– Remedy that comes from inspiration.

The dream is an ingredient;
Content, the metaphor
Generated in the yeast of intuition.

Tenderness invades
The stanza of the stanza,
Spice up the heat of emotion.

Everything is fantasy.
Really is the poem
That drips from the pity
And neutralizes the bitter loneliness.

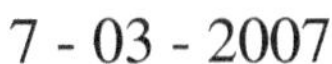

7 - 03 - 2007

DRª ELZA TEIXEIRA

Irvalda and I thank you
From "ADRIEL" kind shipment,
Your book we now read
And it is a tasty read to bessa.

———————

April 5 - 2007

MEMORY PULLS A WORD

Memory pull

A word,

A fact,

And you may have, at that moment,

A sad story.

Pull again another word.

And then,

By the whims of luck,

Through the back and forth of life,

By the multifarious reserves of the unconscious,

You will enjoy, who knows,

From an affable memory

Of fights and victories.

May 30 - 2007

JOÃO QUINTINO SILVA

TIQUINHO OF VERSE

It has value to me,
It's funny and warm
A simple nod,
Handshake
That, even small,
Reveals a brother.

———————

August 3 - 2007

TO THE DESEMBARGADOR
JOSÉ AMÂNCIO DE SOUZA
(A BROTHER IN THE RIMAS)

My dear colleague AMÂNCIO,

GUAPO DESEMBARGADOR,

May the present thunder reach him

In health, peace and love.

Your August Message

– Gesture in which the soul unfurls –

Planted smile on my face,

It made my IRVALDA happy.

Thanks partner!

The attention it gives us

Makes the world enjoyable

And the most beautiful living yet!

August 21 - 2007

JOÃO QUINTINO SILVA

MY KINGDOM FOR A MINI VERSE

Why not
A verse my,
Little one,
Squeezed in a drop of inspiration?

A verse thus of tenderness,
Of good will;
That little that says it all,
Synthesis of magic,
Lint of any atom;
That little thing,
Concentrated,
Microscopic
Able, however,
To explode in cascades of love.

———————

September 8 - 2007

I ENTERED ARCÁDIA AFTER ALL
(The Zeni of Barros Lana)

Unbeatable ZENI,
Great Lady of Poetry,
Your card, which I received,
It was a cause of joy to me!

Thank you, sister-poet,
By the kind of message,
This lyric needs
That praises my image!

I joined ARCÁDIA, after all,
– A garden of pleasant flowers
What an honor the national framework
Of Poets and Writers.

Thank you once again!
I put in this rhyme,
In the emotion that is too much for me,
My hug and my esteem.

————

September 12 - 2007

João Quintino Silva

A BOY'S OBSERVATIONS

How much wrinkle
There's the tortoise!

The ant
Intrigued
With you
And the cockroach
It got boring
Under one foot.

The grasshopper
Climbed on the boy's leg.

Watering
My beanstalk.
When big, it starts up and delivers
to serve at the meal.

House the monkey
With the monkey,
The cow steer,
The ladybug with nobody,
The goat...
– With whom?

If good water is lacking
In a pond,
The fish dies,
The frog runs,
The tree frog
Dry.

2 - October - 2007

AND THEN?

Dear Judge
JOSÉ AMÂNCIO DE SOUZA,
Man of pride and attitude,
Poet, composer,
I only ask you one thing:
How are art and health?

—————

24 - 10 - 2007

FATALITY

The falling leaf
In the stone field
Reminds me of a crush
That had my father.

The damage it did
It was big and so serious
That flight without a ship
There was not again.

---

4 - 11 - 2007

THE DESEMBARGADOR IS INSPIRED

DR. AMÂNCIO DE SOUZA,
Which judges miscellaneous deeds,
Several nights don't even rest,
Making vows and verses.

The precious inspiration
For the musical pieces
He owes her to loneliness
From nocturnal backwaters.

When, then, the Muse cheers him up,
Beautiful corner is printed,
With heat in each rhyme
And emotion in every verse.

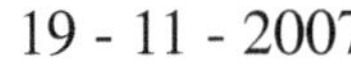

19 - 11 - 2007

Jоãо Quintino Silva

THE DONA INHAZITA ARTIST

The Artist Dona INHAZITA,
With brush and hand paint,
Make up screen so beautiful
That deserves exposure.

When I visited her one day,
Fulfilling a ritual friend,
For the present, which I loved,
I brought one of them with me.

I beg in every prayer,
In the late afternoon,
That the GOOD GOD that does not forget me
Bless you, protect and keep it.

---

26 - November - 2007

UTOPIA

Firstly, the careful and proud pregnancy
In this matrix of every human race
That is a precious home for the fetus.

Then... the light, the throbbing life
Which is briefly summarized
Which soap bubble disperses in the air.

Integration in an always beautiful world,
Peace, health, aging smiling
How those who are happy smile,

Here's a dream... free projection
Of a magician living without frustration,
Without the fear of death and so many crises.

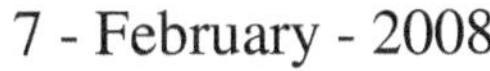

7 - February - 2008

João Quintino Silva

DIVAGING
THE AFTERNOON SHADE

At least one verse
It's heaven
If my soul reaps it.

Pen is trouble
In search of the verse
That lies deep inside
From the soul – this well.

A handful of letters - the word.
And the word overthrows an empire,
Unite two beings,
Makes love everlasting.
And if of God,
It gives substance to the world,
Create the universe.

———————

March 24 - 2008

LOVE, WHAT CAN

Love the weather,
That kiss makes room,
Inspire the measure
From one verse, a rhyme.

———————

24 - 3 - 2008

IN INTIMACY

– That's it, my love, this affliction,
This crazy posture that you love me,
With which you hold me, with which you spill on me
Kisses by the thousand in an unholy anointing?!

Questions. And I, taking your hand,
Bodies intertwined in a bed,
I say smiling, O generous lady:
– It's the heart, honey... it's the heart!

———

May 22 - 2008

THE GENERAL
THE PRESIDENT
DR. FERNANDO BRANDÃO
ARCHBISHOP DOM WALMOR

I went to the HISTORICAL INSTITUTE

Where is King DOCTOR BRANDÃO

That, solicitous and euphoric,

It was soon opening the session.

Invited to the table, O fado,

To Judge Doorgal,

A very cultured prelate

And a handsome general!

Having a GENERAL aside,

D'outro, the CONSECRATED CHURCH,

THE PRESIDENT, after all,

It stood BETWEEN THE CROSS AND THE SWORD!

August 15 - 2008

FLATTERING VERSES

Toast to my sweet little IRVALDA,
The woman of my loves,
To whom I pass written page
Where the verse mimics flowers.

There are more beautiful than IRVALDA,
That is always enchanting,
Much more than emerald?
I answer: no, there is not!

———

9 - 11 - 2008

PLAYING RHYMES

Bahia gives Bahia,
Six ships, one fleet.
Cuiabá gives cuiabano.
Each river, an islet.

Sweet IRVALDA, Agile Girl,
Who was born in a Christian home,
Don't mind the fate
To be from the Leo sign.

She is a candid blonde angel,
A lovely creature
Who has a heart of gold
And soul full of tenderness.

In French, which it adopts,
Bring the Creed to the tongue.
Poor knock on her door,
It does well, it does not die at the same time.

By your side, like a king,
Sporting airy bearing,
When looking from all over the world,
I am happy, I bless luck.

————

12 - 11 - 2008

TO THE POET
DR. PAULO GERALDO CORREA,
IN YOUR AFTERNOON OF AUTHORS

Whose mother is GUARACIABA
And, by father, a MOURA OSCAR,
It has value that is not over
And a heart of envy.

Who has beside IRACEMA,
A love of green years,
Solve any theorem,
Life flows without mistakes.

Who has in the home that commands
With a discreet pride
MÔNICA, PAULO, FERNANDA,
It has a complete treasure.

Coming trance more than perfect,
Composes books, with verses of law:
"A THOUSAND LOVE CONFESSIONS ON LAW"
AND "LOVE LETTERS THAT I DID NOT SEND TO YOU."

———

4 - 2 - 2009

AT LAUNCH OF
"LOVE CONFESSIONS
ON THE RIGHT "

PAULO GERALDO, the Doctor
That also CORRÊA signs,
Verses makes with such vigor
That thrills thin people.

THE DOCTOR. PAULO GERALDO,
Having the Muses back up,
Invented new style
To make poetic art
Bringing law and dialectics together
In poetry for the people.

Your book – JURISPOEMAS –
Treats how many problems
They appear in law.
It gathers loves and doctrines
In cerebrine stanzas
Made, like that, in another way.

Different in the reasons,
His verses avenge the sieves
The most critical process.
So in one voice,
The "LIVE!" Of us all
Along with best wishes!

____

4 - February - 2009

ADMONISH THE FRIEND

DOCTOR AMÂNCIO SOUZA,
Who I saw very often,
Time does not say anything,
If you are doing well, if you are healthy.

How can you friends
Forget the gift of rhyme,
The pleasure of a song
In response to such esteem?

———————

March 2 - 2009

FRUSTRATION

(To Dr. Paulo Geraldo Correa)

JOSE MÁRIO protruded

From the pregnancy of MARY and JOHN.

I would be a doctor growing up,

A surgeon

Famous

And beloved.

One day...

JOSE MÁRIO didn't have a day,

– Born dead.

---

8 - 3 - 2,009

CHILDHOOD

This one I don't overcome,
That in the verse life bases,
Seek Sometimes a Refuge
Inside the house itself.

When girl
– Proceed not adopted –
Throw the doll in a corner
To play somersault.

In the green enchanted valley,
Stage of your childhood,
Night and day – angel taken –
Just did a peraltice.

———————

12 - 3 - 2009

ALWAYS FRIEND

DOCTOR AMÂNCIO SOUZA,
What poetry does so well,
Do not forget a thing:
The friendship you have for me.

And my soul finally rests
By knowing fully
That friend AMÂNCIO SOUZA
Goes well, wastes health.

Tuned in health and verve,
The size of the art continues,
Behold, the Muse that serves him
It accompanies you everywhere.

Your newly recorded CD,
– Codename "GOLD BOWL" –
Having listened with pleasure,
I will keep it as a treasure.

It will be income that sustains
MANGABINHA, the accordion player,
Being enchanting while we are
And that thrills you as an artist.

17 - 3 - 2,009

DESEMBARGADOR JOSÉ AMÂNCIO CORRECTS ME MISCONCEPTION

Oh happy, happy the poet
That in the plots of composing,
Own can hand aesthetic
From an attentive reviewer!

Both facts and aesthetics
Property is guaranteed
In function of dialectic
Of emotion and will.

Your warning, Poet friend,
From the cruel mistake healing the fever,
Warned me of danger
Eating cat by hare.

———————

26 - 3 - 2,009

IN THE SILENCE THAT BECOMES,
AN INTERPELLATION

PROFESSOR GERALDO LIMA,
Da Oliveira where I lived,
Time does not cheer up
Writing me a word!

How can a person
Like Brother GERALDO LIMA
Not have a good sentence
In response to such esteem?

– Dona LÚCIA, what do you tell us?
What good news do we have?
Health guard? Is happy?
As for the children, all well?

———

March 28 - 2009

OTIUM CUM DIGNITATE

DOCTOR AMÂNCIO is quiet,
Enjoying a rest.
Who fulfilled your project,
Judicating all the time,
Well deserves this backwater,
The "warrior's home".

———

March 29 - 2009

CHEESE BREAD
FOOD OF THE GODS

CHEESE BREAD – delicious!

FRIENDSHIP – rare jewel ...

GRATITUDE – a firstfruit

From the soul into the most expensive emotion.

Not any CHEESE BREAD

That gives a good treat,

But what comes out of the way

From MADAME MADALENA.

I felt the still life,

Tasting this delicacy

That with earthenware tea,

It was the charm of my day.

————

2 - April - 2,009

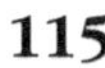

JOÃO QUINTINO SILVA

IF I GOT THE POST?

Yes! In hands, for my sake,
"THE SWAN SONG" - the work
What from NELSON LEITE came
With quality to spare.

I like what is good and beautiful.
I love book that delight
Like this one that came out of print
From NELSON FERREIRA LEITE.

In good tone, "SWAN SONG"
Made of the dear DEPUTY,
Without anything in it,
A consecrated Chronicler.

Closing this message
– Fact I don't forget
And that I accuse with courage –
The book came, the price was missing.

––––––––––

March 29 - 2009

TWO WEIGHTS AND TWO MEASURES

Pay attention, pay close attention
As far as I reveal and can be accepted:
"FERNANDO ANTÔNIO XAVIER BRANDÃO"
Makes a perfect decalsyllable.

From OLAVO BRAZ MARTINS OF GUIMARÃES BILAC,
Who made poetry for adult and boy,
Which is among the most famous Parnassian poets,
Showy name makes complete Alexandrian.

Both are names of rare grandeur.
Framing first class aesthetes.
One – Parnassian worship, expensive jewelry;
The other – fine expression of Minas art.

April 16 - 2009

MOTHER,
THE TREASURE

It is vain to look elsewhere
But may the greater MOTHER be.
There is no good worth so much
Like the MOTHER who is all ours.

———————

20 - 4 - 2,009

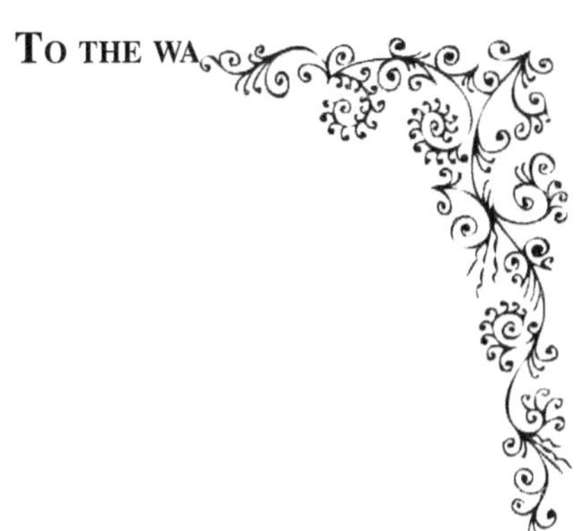

ACROSTIC
TO TÉLCIA

TÉLCIA, value vate,

I got excited about your poem,

Beautiful, full of heat

Like a sun – golden gem –

Imputing beautiful gestures

To dad HERMON VASCONCELOS.

———

28 - 4 - 2,009

João Quintino Silva

OF THE
DR. EUGÊNIO FERRAZ
IN ARCADIA OF MINAS GENERAL

To confess I can
One very bad thing:
– DR. EUGÊNIO FERRAZ
He took possession, and I didn't come here.

CONGRATULATIONS to him and Grêmio
By this lucky step.
For EUGÊNIO, possession is a prize;
To the ARCÁDIA – a strong light.

I tell the righteous president,
DR. MARCO AURÉLIO BAGGIO,
That attacked me, strongly,
A flu without an omen.

This bad flu
It prevented my presence,
Made me a zero, a nothing
Until convalescence comes.

I'm grippy, without complex...
In this sea, I don't drown.
I am not a genuflected man.
Damn dog, I'll heal soon!

———

June 6 - 2009

MERCÊS MARIA MOREIRA, PRECIOUS LADY OF LETTERS

Proclaim I will one day,

In a soiree for poetry,

What MERCÊS LOPES MOREIRA,

Of very rich achievements

And beautiful metaphors,

She is a poet of the first.

PARAOPEBA Natural,

Decanted the land early

With your gifts for poetry.

In Portuguese Casting,

So many beautiful verses made

For beautiful is how much it creates.

The poems you wrote

Honeycombs are like honey,

Of uncontroversial flavor,

Whose splendid reading

The creature reveals us

That was born to make verse.

---

26 - 6 - 2,009

KID POET

A minimal verse,

Monosyllabic,

Syllabic,

Visible only to the eyes of the heart.

From the poet kid

Only expected

A verse tactic,

– TNT pill,

A condensed force

That in the heat of the verve

Explodes into shears of emotion.

———

2 - 07 - 2,009

TO THE CHRONICLER
NELSON FERREIRA LEITE

NELSON LEITE is not bird,

Neither is pain to her mild life.

But on an acute or serious theme,

How good of a beak and pity!

Launched his "SWAN SONG"

Without me being there.

No addiction to it there is that swan

The pleasure the reader feels.

CONGRATULATIONS again to the wizard

From the narrative pen

That transforms the vague fact

In such a living chronicle.

July 5 - 2009

TWO ARTISTS

A footwear:
Art of God,
Art of man.
– Woman.

——————

4 - 09 - 2,009

João **Quintino Silva** served as a teacher in the cities of Uberaba, Uberlândia, Nova Ponte, Monte Alegre, Belo Vale and Monte Carmelo, in the latter holding the role of Director of the "Juscelino Kubitschek" College at the same time. He taught at the Faculty of Law of Sete Lagoas, eventually, and in preparatory courses for competitions.

In this step, it should be noted that **João Quintino** was not only a teacher, but an educator, that is, one who forges the soul of youth with his examples of dignity and ethical posture.

Career judge, he served as magistrate in the Minas Gerais counties of Belo Vale, Campina Verde, Iturama, Oliveira and Belo Horizonte. He was part of the extinct Court of Appeals and was elevated to the high post of Judge at the Egregious Court of Justice of Minas Gerais. In all his decisions, balance and common sense prevailed, as he knows very well that, as Pius XII emphasized, "Justice opus pax".

www.ingramcontent.com/pod-product-compliance
Lightning Source LLC
Chambersburg PA
CBHW071332140726
47996CB00005B/1937